18

STUDY GUIDE

International Relations: To What Extent Was the League of Nations a Success?

CIE

app
available

Published by Clever Lili Limited.

contact@cleverlili.com

First published 2020

ISBN 978-1-913887-17-9

Cover by: Bruce Collection, National Archives of Australia on Wikimedia Commons

Icons by: flaticon and freepik

Contributors: Jonathan Boyd, Lynn Harkin, Megan Quirk, Nicola Nicholls, Jen Mellors

Edited by Paul Connolly and Rebecca Parsley

Design by Evgeni Veskov and Will Fox

DISCOVER MORE OF OUR IGCSE HISTORY STUDY GUIDES

GCSEHistory.com and Clever Lili

CIE

STUDY GUIDE

International Relations:
Were the Peace Treaties of 1919-23 Fair?

GCSEHistory.com

17

CIE

STUDY GUIDE

International Relations:
Why Had International Peace Collapsed by 1939?

GCSEHistory.com

19

CIE

STUDY GUIDE

International Relations:
Who Was to Blame for the Cold War?

GCSEHistory.com

20

CIE

STUDY GUIDE

International Relations:
How Effectively Did the United States Contain the Spread of Communism?

GCSEHistory.com

21

CIE

STUDY GUIDE

International Relations:
How Secure Was the USSR's Control Over Eastern Europe, 1948 - 1989?

GCSEHistory.com

22

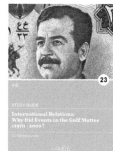

CIE

STUDY GUIDE

International Relations:
Why Did Events in the Gulf Matter c1970 - 2000?

GCSEHistory.com

23

CIE

STUDY GUIDE

The United States, 1919 - 1941

GCSEHistory.com

32

CIE

STUDY GUIDE

The First World War, 1914 - 1918

GCSEHistory.com

31

CIE

STUDY GUIDE

Russia, 1905 - 1941

GCSEHistory.com

33

CIE

STUDY GUIDE

Germany, 1918 - 1945

GCSEHistory.com

34

CIE

STUDY GUIDE

China, c1930-1990

GCSEHistory.com

46

THE GUIDES ARE EVEN BETTER WITH OUR GCSE/IGCSE HISTORY WEBSITE APP AND MOBILE APP

GCSE History is a text and voice web and mobile app that allows you to easily revise for your GCSE/IGCSE exams wherever you are - it's like having your own personal GCSE history tutor. Whether you're at home or on the bus, GCSE History provides you with thousands of convenient bite-sized facts to help you pass your exams with flying colours. We cover all topics - with more than 120,000 questions - across the Edexcel, AQA and CIE exam boards.

GCSEHistory.com

GET IT ON
Google Play

Download on the
App Store

Contents

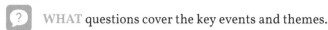

In this study guide, you will see a series of icons, highlighted words and page references. The key below will help you quickly establish what these mean and where to go for more information.

Icons

WHAT questions cover the key events and themes.

WHO questions cover the key people involved.

WHEN questions cover the timings of key events.

WHERE questions cover the locations of key moments.

WHY questions cover the reasons behind key events.

HOW questions take a closer look at the way in which events, situations and trends occur.

IMPORTANCE questions take a closer look at the significance of events, situations, and recurrent trends and themes.

DECISIONS questions take a closer look at choices made at events and situations during this era.

Highlighted words

Abdicate - occasionally, you will see certain words highlighted within an answer. This means that, if you need it, you'll find an explanation of the word or phrase in the glossary which starts on **page 48**.

Page references

Tudor *(p.7)* - occasionally, a certain subject within an answer is covered in more depth on a different page. If you'd like to learn more about it, you can go directly to the page indicated.

The title of the second unit of the Core Content Option B in the CIE History IGCSE is 'To what extent was the League of Nations a success?' This unit investigates the role, structure and success of the League of Nations in the 1920s and 1930s.

Purpose
This unit focuses on international relations and the way in which different nation states interacted, and the change, continuity and significance of their relationships over time. You will study their priorities, agreements, disagreements and the key events that affected them.

Enquiries
This unit gives you the information you need to understand the following:

- The success and failures of the League in the 1920s.
- How far weaknesses in the League's organisation made failure inevitable.
- How far the Depression made the work of the League more difficult.
- The success and failures of the League in the 1930s.

Topics
Topics covered in this course include:

- The birth of the League.
- The structure and organisation of the League.
- The successes and failures of the League commissions.
- Successes and failures of the League in settling the international disputes of the 1920s.
- The impact of the Depression on the work of the League.
- The Treaty of St Germain with Austria.
- The failures of the League in the 1930s, including the Manchurian Crisis, the Abyssinian Crisis and the World Disarmament Conference.

Key Individuals
Key individuals studied in this course include:

- Woodrow Wilson.
- Fridtjof Nansen.
- Ludwik Rajchman.
- Albert Thomas.
- Lord Lytton.
- Benito Mussolini.
- Haile Selassie.

Assessment
This unit usually appears as one of four possible questions in Option B Core Content International Relations Since 1919 on the Paper 1 exam, of which you must complete two. Therefore, you will answer one question on the success of the League of Nations, if this appears as an option on your exam paper. The question is comprised of 3 sections - a, b and c. However, check with your teacher to find out whether this unit will appear on the Paper 2 source paper in your exam.

- On the Paper 1 exam, you may choose to complete a three-part question on this topic, which will be divided into sections a, b and c.
- Question a is worth 4 marks. This question requires you to describe key features of the time period. You will be asked to recall 2 relevant points and support them with details or provide at least four relevant points without supporting detail.
- Question b is worth 6 marks. This question requires you to explain a key event or development. You will need to identify two reasons, support those reasons with relevant factual detail and then explain how the reasons made the event occur.

Quizzes, amazing exam preparation tools and more at GCSEHistory.com

⚬ Question c is worth 10 marks. This question requires you to construct an argument to support and challenge an interpretation stated in the question. You will need to have a minimum of three explanations in total (two on one side and one on the other), fully evaluate the argument and come to a justified conclusion. You will have the opportunity to show your ability to explain and analyse historical events using 2nd order concepts such as causation, consequence, change, continuity, similarity and difference.

⚬ If this topic appears on Paper 2, you will answer six questions on a range of source material about this topic. Check with your teacher to find out your Paper 2 topic.

Revision! A dreaded word. Everyone knows it's coming, everyone knows how much it helps with your exam performance, and everyone struggles to get started! We know you want to do the best you can in your IGCSEs, but schools aren't always clear on the best way to revise. This can leave students wondering:

- ✔ How should I plan my revision time?
- ✔ How can I beat procrastination?
- ✔ What methods should I use? Flash cards? Re-reading my notes? Highlighting?

Luckily, you no longer need to guess at the answers. Education researchers have looked at all the available revision studies, and the jury is in. They've come up with some key pointers on the best ways to revise, as well as some thoughts on popular revision methods that aren't so helpful. The next few pages will help you understand what we know about the best revision methods.

How can I beat procrastination?

This is an age-old question, and it applies to adults as well! Have a look at our top three tips below.

◎ Reward yourself

When we think a task we have to do is going to be boring, hard or uncomfortable, we often put if off and do something more 'fun' instead. But we often don't really enjoy the 'fun' activity because we feel guilty about avoiding what we should be doing. Instead, get your work done and promise yourself a reward after you complete it. Whatever treat you choose will seem all the sweeter, and you'll feel proud for doing something you found difficult. Just do it!

◎ Just do it!

We tend to procrastinate when we think the task we have to do is going to be difficult or dull. The funny thing is, the most uncomfortable part is usually making ourselves sit down and start it in the first place. Once you begin, it's usually not nearly as bad as you anticipated.

◎ Pomodoro technique

The pomodoro technique helps you trick your brain by telling it you only have to focus for a short time. Set a timer for 20 minutes and focus that whole period on your revision. Turn off your phone, clear your desk, and work. At the end of the 20 minutes, you get to take a break for five. Then, do another 20 minutes. You'll usually find your rhythm and it becomes easier to carry on because it's only for a short, defined chunk of time.

Spaced practice

We tend to arrange our revision into big blocks. For example, you might tell yourself: "This week I'll do all my revision for the Cold War, then next week I'll do the Medicine Through Time unit."

This is called **massed practice**, because all revision for a single topic is done as one big mass.

But there's a better way! Try **spaced practice** instead. Instead of putting all revision sessions for one topic into a single block, space them out. See the example below for how it works.

This means planning ahead, rather than leaving revision to the last minute - but the evidence strongly suggests it's worth it. You'll remember much more from your revision if you use **spaced practice** rather than organising it into big blocks. Whichever method you choose, though, remember to reward yourself with breaks.

Spaced practice (more effective):

week 1	week 2	week 3	week 4
Topic 1	Topic 1	Topic 1	Topic 1
Topic 2	Topic 2	Topic 2	Topic 2
Topic 3	Topic 3	Topic 3	Topic 3
Topic 4	Topic 4	Topic 4	Topic 4

Massed practice (less effective)

week 1	week 2	week 3	week 4
Topic 1	Topic 2	Topic 3	Topic 4

What methods should I use to revise?

Self-testing/flash cards

Self explanation/mind-mapping

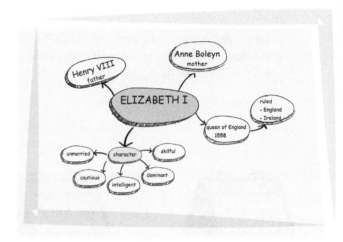

The research shows a clear winner for revision methods - **self-testing**. A good way to do this is with **flash cards**. Flash cards are really useful for helping you recall short – but important – pieces of information, like names and dates.

Side A - question

Side B - answer

Write questions on one side of the cards, and the answers on the back. This makes answering the questions and then testing yourself easy. Put all the cards you get right in a pile to one side, and only repeat the test with the ones you got wrong - this will force you to work on your weaker areas.

pile with right answers

pile with wrong answers

As this book has a quiz question structure itself, you can use it for this technique.

Another good revision method is **self-explanation**. This is where you explain how and why one piece of information from your course linked with another piece.

This can be done with **mind-maps**, where you draw the links and then write explanations for how they connect. For example, President Truman is connected with anti-communism because of the Truman Doctrine.

Quizzes, amazing exam preparation tools and more at GCSEHistory.com

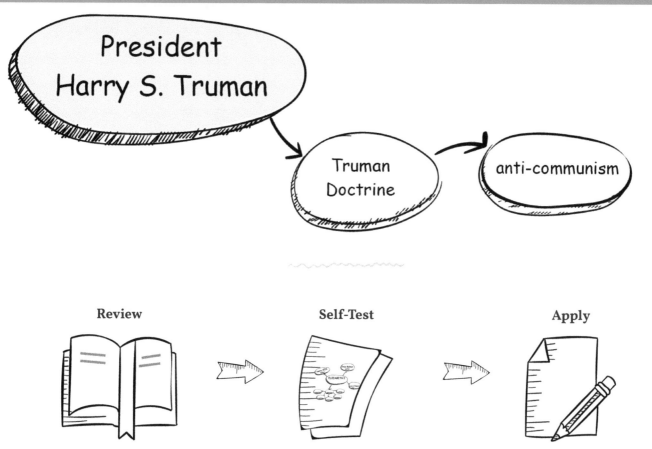

Review

Start by highlighting or re-reading to create your flashcards for self-testing.

Self-Test

Test yourself with flash cards. Make mind maps to explain the concepts.

Apply

Apply your knowledge on practice exam questions.

Which revision techniques should I be cautious about?

Highlighting and **re-reading** are not necessarily bad strategies - but the research does say they're less effective than flash cards and mind-maps.

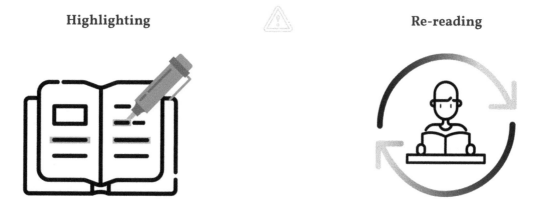

Highlighting

Re-reading

If you do use these methods, make sure they are **the first step to creating flash cards**. Really engage with the material as you go, rather than switching to autopilot.

THE LEAGUE OF NATIONS

TIMELINE

8th January - Woodrow Wilson outlined the idea of the League of Nations in his '14 Points speech' *(p.14)*

1918

1919

January - Clashes in Teschen *(p.26)*

1920

10th January - Official inauguration (opening) of the League of Nations *(p.14)*

March - US Congress defeated proposal to join the League for the second time *(p.14)*

April - Vilna seized by Poland *(p.27)*

1921

March - Upper Silesia plebiscite *(p.29)*

June - Aaland Islands Settlement *(p.28)*

1922

February - Washington Naval Agreement *(p.35)*

April - Rapallo Pact *(p.36)*

1923

January - French invasion of the Ruhr *(p.30)*

September - Withdrawal of Italian troops from Corfu *(p.30)*

1924

July - A League commission rules on Mosul *(p.32)*

1925

October - Border clash between Greece and Bulgaria *(p.33)*

December - Locarno Pact *(p.37)*

1928

August - Kellogg-Briand Pact *(p.34)*

1929

October - Wall Street Crash, leading to global depression *(p.40)*

1931

September - Japanese invasion of Manchuria *(p.41)*

1932

February - World Disarmament Conference began *(p.43)*

September - Lytton report on Manchuria *(p.41)*

1933

February - Japan left the League of Nations and invaded the Jehol province *(p.41)*

November - Germany left the League of Nations *(p.14)*

1934

September - USSR joined League *(p.14)*

1935

October - Italian invasion of Abyssinia *(p.44)*

December - Hoare-Laval Pact *(p.44)*

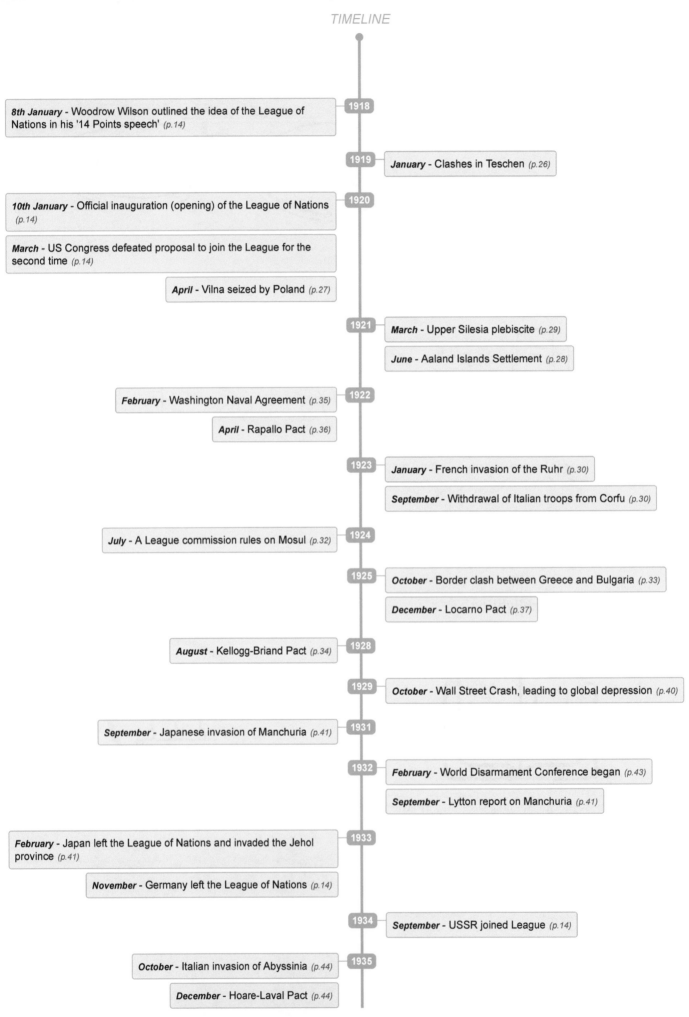

Quizzes, amazing exam preparation tools and more at GCSEHistory.com

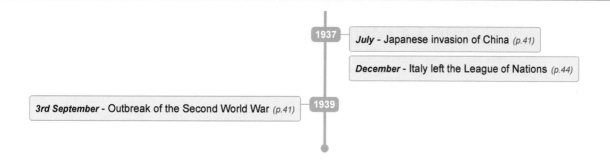

1937

July - Japanese invasion of China *(p.41)*

December - Italy left the League of Nations *(p.44)*

3rd September - Outbreak of the Second World War *(p.41)* **1939**

THE LEAGUE OF NATIONS

'You will say, "Is the League an absolute guaranty against war?" No; I do not know any absolute guaranty against the errors of human judgment or the violence of human passions...' Woodrow Wilson

What was the League of Nations?

The League of Nations was an international organisation that aimed to make the world more peaceful. It provided a platform for countries to solve the issues that might lead to war.

Whose idea was the League of Nations?

There were 3 important individuals that put the League of Nations together.

- ☑ President Wilson originally drafted his ideas about the League of Nations in his 14 Points at the end of the First World War.
- ☑ Jan Smuts of South Africa was involved in the discussions, as was British politician Sir Robert Cecil.
- ☑ British prime minister David Lloyd George also contributed to the talks.

What were the aims of the League of Nations?

The League of Nations had a number of aims.

- ☑ Its primary aim was to keep world peace, and solve disputes that might lead to war.
- ☑ It wanted to achieve world disarmament.
- ☑ It wanted to achieve global co-operation in trade.
- ☑ It aimed to improve the lives of people worldwide.

When was the League of Nations formed?

The League of Nations came into being in January 1920.

Where was the League of Nations based?

The League of Nations was based in Geneva, Switzerland. Switzerland was seen as a peaceful country and was also home to the headquarters of the Red Cross.

What was the Covenant of the League of Nations?

The Covenant of the League of Nations was the name chosen by President Wilson to describe the League's constitution. It contained 26 articles, or laws, about how the League should be organised.

What were the problems with setting up the League of Nations?

The politicians who were responsible for setting up the League encountered some problems.

- ☑ The plans for the League were put together in a hurry.
- ☑ Critics felt the aims of the organisation were badly-defined or too idealistic.
- ☑ Britain wanted a simpler organisation that would only meet in emergencies, similar to the existing Conference of Ambassadors which oversaw the fulfilment of the peace settlement of the First World War.
- ☑ France wanted a strong league with its own army.
- ☑ American Congress decided the USA should not join the League.
- ☑ Other countries, such as the USSR and Germany, were not invited to join.

Why didn't the USA join the League of Nations?

There were 6 reasons the USA did not join the League of Nations.

- The idea of the League of Nations was unpopular in the USA.
- Many Americans, particularly those with German ancestry, hated the Treaty of Versailles. They did not want membership of an organisation set up to enforce it.
- After the casualties of the First World War, many Americans were afraid their soldiers would become involved in conflicts not directly related to America.
- The League's sanctions might hurt American trade.
- There were fears the League would be used to defend the British and French empires. Many Americans were anti-imperialist.
- Wilson was too ill to run for re-election in 1920 but the Republican candidate, Warren Harding, campaigned for American isolationism and a return to 'normalcy'. These ideas appealed to the electorate, who voted him in.

What did Britain think of the League of Nations?

David Lloyd George was critical of the League to being with. However, in March 1919 he issued the Fontainebleau Memorandum which gave it his full support.

What made Britain change its opinion the League of Nations?

The League was to run German colonies lost under the Treaty of Versailles as mandates. Historians have argued Britain saw this an an empire-building opportunity.

What did France think of the League of Nations?

France was supportive of any measure that would protect them from another German invasion.

How was the League of Nations organised?

The League was organised into 7 bodies that had different roles within it.

- The Secretariat.
- The Assembly *(p. 19)* of the League.
- The Council of the League *(p. 19)*.
- The Permanent Court of International Justice.
- The International Labour Organisation *(p.21)*.
- The Commissions.
- A Council of Ambassadors existed between 1920 and 1931.

What were the weaknesses of the League of Nations?

The League had 7 weaknesses that meant it struggled to be effective.

- The USA was never a member of the League. It became isolationist after the Paris Peace Conference, meaning the League didn't have America's powerful and influential support.
- Germany wasn't allowed to join the League until 1926, which meant the organisation looked like a 'winner's club'. Germany left in 1933 after Adolf Hitler came to power.
- Soviet Russia wasn't invited to join the League until 1934, because it was communist.
- Along with France, Britain was one of the League's most influential and powerful members. However, it was mostly concerned with its empire rather than prioritising the League's principles.
- Along with Britain, France was one of the League's most influential and powerful members. However, the country was worried about maintaining its security against potential German aggression, rather than prioritising the League's principles.
- The League was slow to reach decisions as its Assembly *(p. 19)* only met once a year.
- The League had to rely on members donating their armies, as it didn't have its own. This made it weak against aggression.

☑ All decisions in the League had to be unanimous, so each country had an equal say. This meant just one country could veto an action being taken.

 ## What was collective security in the League of Nations?

Collective security was the principle on which the League of Nations worked. It was based on the idea that if all members worked together, they could force any aggressive country to stop threatening the peace.

 ## What was collective security in the League of Nations also known as?

It was known as Article 10 in the Covenant of the League.

 ## What were the powers of the League of Nations?

The League had three main powers at its disposal to keep the peace, based on the principles of collective security.

☑ Moral disapproval (also known as condemnation). If the Council voted to condemn the action of a country, it knew the weight of the world's opinion was on the League's side.

☑ Economic sanctions. If a country was aggressive, the Council could decide that League members would refuse to trade with it or lend it money. This is also known as being 'blacklisted'.

☑ Military sanctions. As a last resort, the Council could decide to send in an army of soldiers from member states.

 ## Who were members of the League of Nations?

The League had many countries as members, but there were also some important non-members.

☑ The League had 42 member countries when it was first set up, and 59 by the end of the 1930s.

☑ The USA was never a member of the League, even though it was US president Woodrow Wilson's idea.

☑ In the absence of the USA, Britain and France were the most dominant and influential members of the League.

☑ Germany was allowed to join in 1926, but left to rearm in secret shortly after Hitler was appointed chancellor in 1933.

☑ The USSR was allowed to join in 1934.

☑ Japan, a permanent member of the Council of the League (p.19), left in 1933 after the Manchurian Crisis (p.41).

☑ Italy, a permanent member of the Council of the League (p.19), left in 1937 after the Abyssinian (p.44) Crisis.

 ## What were the League of Nations' successes in the 1920s?

During the 1920s, the League saw some significant successes.

☑ It successfully solved disputes in the Aaland Islands (p.28), Teschen (p.26), Mosul (p.32) and Bulgaria.

☑ The League largely changed the way countries dealt with one another, handled problems, and solved global disputes.

☑ The League gave confidence to smaller nations which could not protect themselves.

☑ The League was successful in rebuilding post-war Europe.

☑ The World Health Organisation ran many successful campaigns and set up research institutes.

☑ The Refugees' Commission successfully repatriated thousands of prisoners of war.

☑ The International Labour Organisation (p.21) began to pave the way for workers' rights, offering a minimum wage and suggested work hours.

☑ The Slavery Commission worked to get rid of slavery and prostitution globally.

☑ The Economic and Financial Committee sent experts to help countries such as Austria and Hungary, whose economies were nearly bankrupt.

☑ The other commissions worked to improve life for people across the world.

 ## What were the League of Nations' failures in the 1920s?

The League was not completely successful in the 1920s.

☑ Its decisions in disputes over Corfu (p.30) and Vilna (p.27) were seen as unfair, as was its failure to act over the Ruhr.

- ☑ The International Labour Organisation *(p.21)* failed to force countries to introduce better working practices.
- ☑ The failure to disarm other nations was damaging to the League's reputation and caused even more resentment from Germany, which had been forced to disarm.
- ☑ The League showed itself to be biased towards larger, more powerful nations. This was clear during the Corfu *(p.30)* crisis.
- ☑ The League's most powerful members, Britain and France, prioritised their own needs before those of the League.
- ☑ Without an army of its own, the League showed it could only use moral condemnation and sanctions to make a country back down.
- ☑ Some world problems required agreements outside of the League. For example, the Dawes Plan *(p.38)* and the Locarno Pact *(p.37)* demonstrated the League was not fully effective at dealing with the issue of Franco-German relations.

 ## What were the League of Nations' successes in the 1930s?

The League had 2 important achievements in the 1930s:

- ☑ The Saar Commission successfully organised a plebiscite, where the population voted to reunite with Germany in 1935.
- ☑ The League successfully convened 26 nations to combat the dangerous selling of illegal drugs. This still functions today.

 ## What were the League of Nations' failures in the 1930s?

The League's failures in the 1930s far outweighed its successes.

- ☑ With the global Depression after 1929, the League faced many challenges it had not previously encountered.
- ☑ The Japanese invasion of Manchuria in 1931 showed the League was slow to act and powerless. Although the League condemned Japan's actions, it could not do anything to stop them.
- ☑ Following the invasion of Manchuria, the Japanese withdrew from the League and continued to invade other parts of China. This was a huge embarrassment to the organisation.
- ☑ At the Disarmament Conference, Germany walked out early over unfair treatment. Although it later returned, Hitler secretly began to rearm. By October, Germany again withdrew from the conference, and shortly after from the League itself.
- ☑ The Disarmament Conference failed for many reasons, as few members seriously considered disarming. It also saw Britain and France were divided on what to do with Germany.
- ☑ Mussolini's invasion of Abyssinia *(p.44)* in 1935 was the final blow to the League of Nations. Once again it was slow to act and did little to discourage Italian aggression, wanting to retain an ally against Hitler.
- ☑ Equally damaging was the secret deal created by the British and French foreign ministers, Hoare and Laval. They planned to offer Mussolini two thirds of Abyssinia *(p.44)* in return for his withdrawal. They didn't consult the League or the Abyssinian emperor, or seek approval, first.
- ☑ As a result of the Abyssinian *(p.44)* Crisis, the League was viewed as insignificant in international affairs from then on.

 ## What were the League of Nations' overall successes?

The League had mixed success in its lifetime and did solve some disputes in the 1920s. Overall, the League's biggest success came from commissions that sought to fix global issues.

 ## What were the League of Nations' overall failures?

The League fell very short of Wilson's ideal. It was weakened by a lack of key members and an army of its own. This, along with the Depression and the self-interest of France and Britain, meant it was unprepared for dealing with aggressive nations in the 1930s.

 ## What did the different parts of the League of Nations do?

The League consisted of several bodies that each performed a different function:

- ✅ The Secretariat was the League's civil service.
- ✅ The Assembly *(p.19)* was a big meeting of all member countries to make important decisions about the League, and was effectively its parliament.
- ✅ The Council of the League *(p.19)* was a smaller executive body which decided how the League would react to events.
- ✅ The Permanent Court of International Justice was a mostly independent body that reached legal decisions when countries had disputes.
- ✅ The International Labour Organisation *(p.21)* was mostly independent and worked to improve working conditions in all its member countries.
- ✅ The Commissions were agencies set up by the League to tackle specific problems in member countries.
- ✅ The Council of Ambassadors was a group of important diplomats that had existed before the League was created. They represented the allied powers in issues around the peace settlements. It was dissolved in 1931.

DID YOU KNOW?

Woodrow Wilson suffered a serious stroke in October 1919.
This made it difficult for him to continue campaigning for the League.

THE SECRETARIAT

The civil service of the League.

What was the League's Secretariat?

The Secretariat was the League of Nation's *(p.14)* civil service.

How did the League of Nations' Secretariat work?

The Secretariat worked through a body of experts from different areas such as economics, education and health.

Who was involved with the League of Nations' Secretariat?

The work of the Secretariat, led by Eric Drummond between 1920 and 1933, was carried out by international officials from member nations. They were expected to remain neutral in respect of their nations. In 1920, there were 158 civil servants; by 1931 this had increased to 707.

What was the role of the League of Nations' Secretariat?

The role of the Secretariat was to support all other organisations in the League of Nations.

What were the League of Nations' Secretariat duties?

The Secretariat had 2 important duties:

- ✅ It was in charge of administration and organising actions undertaken by the League.
- ✅ It was responsible for carrying out any decisions the League made, except for those on military issues.

What problems did the League of Nations' secretariat face?

The League's Secretariat faced problems because it was expensive to run and grew too large over time.

THE ASSEMBLY OF THE LEAGUE

'The Assembly was created in order that anybody that purposed anything wrong should be subjected to the awkward circumstance that everybody could talk about it.'
Woodrow Wilson

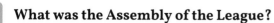

What was the Assembly of the League?

The Assembly of the League of Nations had representatives from each member country and was one of the League's main decision-making bodies.

What did the Assembly do in the League?

The Assembly had 6 important roles:

- ☑ The Assembly controlled the direction and aims of the League.
- ☑ It made decisions about the League's policy and controlled its budget.
- ☑ It decided whether to admit new countries as members.
- ☑ It elected non-permanent members of the Council.
- ☑ It met once a year. Every member country had one vote, which ensured smaller countries had the same powers as larger ones, and no single nation could dominate the League.
- ☑ It was effectively the League's parliament.

THE COUNCIL OF THE LEAGUE

'The Council is the source of every active policy of the League, and no active policy of the League can be adopted without a unanimous vote of the council.'
Woodrow Wilson

What was the Council of the League?

The Council of the League was the executive of the League of Nations.

What did the Council do in the League?

The Council made important decisions for the League of Nations:

- ☑ It met 4 or 5 times a year, and when there was a crisis.
- ☑ It had 4 permanent members in 1920 - Britain, France, Japan and Italy. These might sometimes dominate discussions and decisions.
- ☑ Germany became a permanent member in 1926.
- ☑ It also had between 4 and 11 non-permanent members, who were voted in by the Assembly *(p.19)* at three-year intervals.
- ☑ It could reach decisions and react more quickly than the Assembly *(p.19)* in times of crisis.
- ☑ Votes had to be unanimous, which mean each member of the Council could veto decisions.

DID YOU KNOW?

The number of temporary seats in the Council of the League was increased from 4 to 6 in 1921, and then to 9 in 1926.

THE PERMANENT COURT OF JUSTICE

'To create an organisation which is in a position to protect peace in this world of conflicting interests and egotistic wills is a frighteningly difficult task...'
Swedish politician Hjalmar Branting

What was the Permanent Court of Justice?

The Permanent Court of Justice was the legal body of the League of Nations.

Who was in the Permanent Court of Justice?

It had 11 judges who served for 9 years.

What did the Permanent Court of Justice do?

It provided legal advice to the Council.

Where was the Permanent Court of Justice based?

It was based in the Hague, in the Netherlands.

DID YOU KNOW?

Between 1921 and 1939, the Permanent Court of International Justice made more than 30 official decisions.

THE INTERNATIONAL LABOUR ORGANISATION

'It is the power of the united moral forces of the world.'
Woodrow Wilson

What was the International Labour Organisation?

The International Labour Organisation was the part of the League of Nations that looked into working conditions.

What were the aims of the International Labour Organisation?

It aimed to improve the working conditions of people worldwide.

Who set up the International Labour Organisation?

It was set up by the French socialist, Albert Thomas.

What did the International Labour Organisation do?

The International Labour Organisation took action in the following 6 ways:

- ☑ It consulted with a range of people about working conditions and then gave advice.
- ☑ Each country sent employers, government ministers and workers to discuss working conditions.
- ☑ It collected data and published advice on good working practices, including an eight-hour day, annual holiday with pay, and a minimum working age.
- ☑ It published research into health and safety in the workplace.
- ☑ It made recommendations to governments and employers, but could not make laws.

DID YOU KNOW?

Albert Thomas turned the International Labour Organisation into an institution with more than 400 members.

THE COMMISSIONS

'No League of Nations, or of individuals, can avail, without a change of heart.'
Henry Stephen Salt, 1921

What were the League's Special Commissions?

The Special Commissions were organisations that carried out the League's humanitarian work.

How did the League of Nations' Special Commissions work?

The League's commissions were several different organisations who undertook the humanitarian work needed to tackle issues the League saw as important.

What was the role of the League of Nations' Special Commissions?

The role of the League's Special Commissions was to help people in areas it was particularly worried about. These included tackling issues such as:

- ☑ Working conditions.

- ✅ Health.
- ✅ Human rights abuses.
- ✅ Economic concerns.
- ✅ Harmful drugs.

What different Special Commissions did the League of Nations set up?

The League set up a number of different Special Commissions, including:

- ✅ The Mandates Commission, for supervising the former colonies of Germany and Turkey.
- ✅ The Danzig Commission, which supervised the former German city.
- ✅ The Minorities Commission, which tried to improve the treatment and rights of ethnic minorities.
- ✅ The Special Commission for Drug Traffic, that tried to stop drug smuggling and addiction.
- ✅ The Refugees' Committee, which aimed to solve the problem of refugees and prisoners of war after the First World War.
- ✅ The Health Committee, which aimed to improve the health of people around the world.
- ✅ The Slavery Commission, which aimed to abolish slavery.
- ✅ The Women's Rights Commission, which aimed to introduce better equality for women.
- ✅ The World Disarmament Commission, which aimed to get all countries to reduce their armed forces.
- ✅ Economic and financial commissions were set up to help countries with struggling economies after the First World War.

What was the League of Nations' mandates special commission?

The mandates special commission had the following roles:

- ✅ It was responsible for the colonies of nations defeated in the First World War.
- ✅ It had a team of advisers that checked in on colonies previously owned by nations defeated in the First World War.
- ✅ It reported back on the treatment of the colonies and whether Britain and France, who now ruled them, were treating them fairly.
- ✅ It aimed to ensure France and Britain weren't abusing their authority, but were helping the people of each colony.
- ✅ It also took responsibility for the wellbeing of minority groups.

What was the Refugees Commission in the League of Nations?

The Refugees Commission (or Committee) was set up following the end of the First World War with the aim of repatriating the hundreds of thousands of refugees who had fled areas of conflict.

- ✅ Its main concern was focusing on territories such as the Balkans, Greece, Armenia and Turkey.
- ✅ The League of Nations reported in 1927 that there were 750,000 refugees from former Russian states, and 168,000 Armenians, all in need of repatriation.
- ✅ The League of Nations appointed Fridtjof Nansen to oversee the huge task of repatriating and aiding the refugees.

What was the Slavery Commission in the League of Nations?

The League of Nations created the Slavery Commission to abolish worldwide slavery, and help any worker being treated like a slave.

What was the League of Nations' Commission to prevent drug use?

The League of Nations' Commission to prevent drug use had 3 important aims.

- ✅ The League had a Special Committee for Drug Traffic that aimed to regulate harmful drugs and co-operate on the problem of drug-smuggling.

☑ As part of this, the League set up the Permanent Central Opium Board. This aimed to stop the creation and distribution of opium, a highly addictive drug.

☑ In 1925, the scope of the Permanent Central Opium Board was widened to include the regulation of other drugs.

What was the Health Organisation in the League of Nations' Commissions?

The Health Organisation had 4 important roles.

☑ The Health Organisation, or Committee, aimed to eradicate dangerous diseases and educate the general public on hygiene.

☑ The Health Organisation also worked alongside charities to spread global awareness on major health issues.

☑ It set up medical research projects and centres.

☑ It worked on the prevention of disease.

What problems did the League of Nations' Special Commissions face?

The League had huge ambitions to make the world a fairer and safer place for everyone. They had some success in helping people, but there were also many failures.

DID YOU KNOW?

The League of Nations' charter stated all roles within the organisation should be 'open equally to men and women'.

However, in practice, very few women worked for the League.

THE SUCCESS OF THE COMMISSIONS

'The difficult is what takes a little time. The impossible is what takes a little longer.'
Fridtjof Nansen

What were the successes of the League's commissions?

The League's commissions worked with varying degrees of success in the 1920s.

How successful was the Health Organisation commission in the League of Nations?

The League's Health Organisation was led by Ludwik Rajchman and became one of the most successful commissions. It had 7 main successes during the inter-war years:

☑ It worked with non-League countries, such as the USSR, USA and Germany, as well as member states.

☑ It helped prevent a typhoid epidemic in the Soviet Union with a public education campaign about hygiene.

☑ It began an international campaign to kill mosquitoes and reduced the spread of malaria and yellow fever.

☑ It set up research institutes in London, Copenhagen and Singapore.

☑ It reduced the number of cases of leprosy.

☑ The Health Committee has been acknowledged as one of the most successful aspects of the League of Nations.

☑ After the League of Nations was disbanded, the Health Committee became the World Health Organisation and worked with the United Nations. It still exists today.

How successful was the Refugees Commission in the League of Nations?

The Refugees Commission was run by scientist and explorer Fridtjof Nansen. It had 6 key successes in the inter-war years.

- ☑ It introduced the Nansen Passport to help repatriate prisoners of war and refugees who were stranded in foreign countries.
- ☑ It worked with the Red Cross to help 425,000 people to either return home or to settle in new places.
- ☑ Their methods included finding transport, setting up camps, teaching new trades and skills, and building new settlements.
- ☑ Nansen achieved all this on a shoestring budget, and earned a lot of praise and gratitude for the League.
- ☑ With a refugee crisis in Turkey in 1922, the League worked quickly to make sure camps were set up, and that these were free from diseases such as cholera, smallpox and dysentery.
- ☑ From 1933, there was a League High Commissioner, American James G MacDonald, to help Jewish refugees from Germany. However, he resigned in 1935 over a lack of support from the League.

 How successful was the Economic Commission in the League of Nations?

After the First World War, several countries faced economic problems. The League helped in 4 main ways:

- ☑ In 1922 financial experts drew up a rescue plan to help Austria, which was in danger of financial collapse and bankruptcy following the war.
- ☑ Other rescue programmes were introduced for Hungary, Greece and Bulgaria.
- ☑ The League helped to stabilise economies by taking action on currency and credit.
- ☑ Codes were also developed for importing and exporting so that all members followed the same trading rules.

 How successful was the International Labour Organisation commission in the League of Nations?

The International Labour Organisation (p.21) had 5 major successes and 3 failures:

- ☑ It successfully banned poisonous lead paint from workplaces.
- ☑ It resolved that the working week should be no longer than 48 hours.
- ☑ It improved people's working conditions by helping Greece to set up social security.
- ☑ In the first two years of the ILO (p.21), 16 International Labour Conventions were accepted.
- ☑ In 1928, 77 countries agreed to set a minimum wage.
- ☑ However, it couldn't force countries to follow its ideas and many didn't, including Britain.
- ☑ It failed to help improve working conditions when in 1919 it tried to ban children aged under 14 from working. However, the members did not agree to this as it would cost too much money.
- ☑ In 1935 it tried to limit the working day to 8 hours. However, members voted against the measure as it would be too costly.
- ☑ Nevertheless, it was successful in introducing standards for work and employment and it became increasingly difficult for member states to ignore these.

 What were the successes of thte Slavery Commission in the League of Nations?

The Slavery Commission had 4 successes in the 1920s:

- ☑ It aimed to end slavery, including 'white slavery' - the forcing of women and children into prostitution.
- ☑ It freed 200,000 slaves in Sierra Leone, organising raids on the camps of slave traders. As a result, in 1927, Sierra Leone announced it had abolished slavery.
- ☑ It reduced the death rate in workers on the Tanganyika Railway, from 50% to 4%.
- ☑ It helped to achieve the abolition of slavery in Jordan, Iraq, and Nepal.

How successful was the Disarmament Commission in the League of Nations?

The Disarmament Commission was one of the least successful commissions in the League of Nations.

☑ By the end of the 1920s only the defeated nations had disarmed, and that was solely because they were forced to do so under the terms of the treaties.

☑ In 1922, the Washington Naval Agreement *(p.35)* led to the USA, Britain, France, Japan and Italy agreeing to reduce their naval forces. This decision was later included in the League of Nations treaties.

☑ The Commission was unable to organise a World Disarmament Conference until 1932 because there were so many arguments about technicalities and details.

 ### How successful was the League of Nations commission for drugs?

The League failed to help improve problems with the supply and use of illegal drugs. Few members were interested in tackling the issue as they gained financially from the sale of opium.

DID YOU KNOW?

Fridtjof Nansen, the Norwegian head of the Refugees Commission, had an interesting career.

He was a scientist, a polar explorer, an author, an academic, a humanitarian activist, a diplomat, and a champion skier and ice skater. He also won a Nobel Peace Prize and led the first team to cross the middle of Greenland on cross-country skis.

INTERNATIONAL DISPUTES IN THE 1920S

'The League of Nations is the greatest humbug in history.'
David Lloyd George

 ### What did the League of Nations do to try and keep peace in the 1920s?

In its effort to keep world peace, the League was involved in a number of disputes between nations in the 1920s.

 ### What disputes did the League of Nations get involved in during the 1920s to try and keep the peace?

The League got involved in 8 key disputes in the 1920s, in its efforts to keep peace in the world. These included:

☑ A dispute between Poland and Czechoslovakia over Teschen *(p.26)* in 1919.

☑ A dispute between Poland and Lithuania over Vilna *(p.27)* in 1920.

☑ A dispute between Germany and Poland over Upper Silesia *(p.29)* between 1921 and 1925.

☑ A dispute between Sweden and Finland over the Aland Islands in 1921.

☑ A dispute between Greece and Italy over an incident in Corfu *(p.30)* in 1923.

☑ A dispute between France and Germany over the Ruhr in 1923.

☑ A dispute between Turkey and Iraq with Britain over Mosul *(p.32)* in 1924.

☑ A dispute between Greece and Bulgaria over an incident on the Bulgarian border in 1925.

 ### What actions did the League of Nations take to deal with disputes and keep the peace during the 1920s?

The League used a range of actions to deal with disputes including:

☑ Plebiscites, which were a vote from all members of the electorate on an important issue.

- ☑ The use of experts to investigate an issue.
- ☑ Moral condemnation - which was essentially a good telling-off.
- ☑ Overpowering smaller countries.
- ☑ Using the power of leading members such as Britain and France to deal with disputes.

Why did the League of Nations get involved in dealing with disputes to keep the peace in the 1920s?

There were a number of reasons the League of Nations got involved in various disputes in the 1920s including:

- ☑ The overarching aim of the League of Nations was to prevent future wars.
- ☑ It's aim was to encourage compromise and co-operation and, as the map of Europe was redrawn after the First World War, there were a number of disputes regarding where the borders should be.
- ☑ Some countries were even prepared to go to war, so it was important that the League acted in order to keep the peace.

DID YOU KNOW?

The League did not always get involved in disputes between countries.

In 1920, Poland invaded Russia and forced it to give up 80,000 sq km of land in the Treaty of Riga. The League did nothing.

THE TESCHEN DISPUTE, 1919

Poland and Czechoslovakia fought over the coal-mining region.

What was the Teschen dispute?

The League of Nations became involved in the Teschen dispute in 1919.

Where is Teschen?

Teschen, a coal-mining region, was located between Poland and Czechoslovakia after the break-up of the German and Austro-Hungarian empires.

Who was involved in the Teschen dispute?

Czechoslovakia and Poland both believed they should control Teschen. Around 1,000 people were killed when fighting broke out between them in 1919.

How did the League react to the Teschen dispute?

The League divided the region up between the two countries, with Czechoslovakia gaining most of the coal mines.

What was the result of the Teschen dispute?

The fighting stopped, but Poland refused to accept the decision and bad feeling continued between the two countries until the Second World War.

THE VILNA DISPUTE, 1920

Poland and Lithuania disagree over Lithuania's capital.

What was the Vilna dispute?

The League adjudicated when there was disagreement between Poland and Lithuania in 1920 over Vilna.

Where is Vilna?

Vilna, a large city in the south of Lithuania, was the country's constitutional capital.

Who was involved in the Vilna dispute?

The Vilna dispute occurred between Poland and Lithuania over the city of Vilna.

Why was there a dispute over Vilna?

The Peace Settlement at the end of the First World War saw countries that were part of the Austria-Hungarian empire given independence. New countries were created, including Poland and Lithuania, and the people living in Vilna wanted to be Polish rather than Lithuanian.

How did the League react to the Vilna dispute?

The League told Poland to withdraw its troops when it invaded Vilna but Poland refused. The Council of Ambassadors awarded the city to Poland.

Why didn't the League of Nations uphold the treaties in the Vilna dispute?

France, which was still more concerned with strengthening defences against Germany, didn't want to upset Poland as it was a potential ally. Britain wouldn't send its army without the support of other members.

What was the result of the Vilna dispute?

Lithuania refused to accept the decision, but could do nothing except break off diplomatic relations with Poland until 1938.

What was significant about the Vilna dispute?

The Vilna dispute is a significant event when considering the successes of the League of Nations. The first time the League was asked to settle a dispute, it took no action against the invading country.

THE AALAND ISLANDS DISPUTE, 1921

Finland and Sweden disputed a group of islands located between them.

What was the Aaland Islands dispute?

The League of Nations got involved in a dispute between Finland and Sweden in 1921 over who controlled the Aaland Islands.

Where are the Aaland Islands?

The Aaland Islands are located between Finland and Sweden, in the Baltic Sea.

Who was involved in the dispute over the Aaland Islands?

Finland and Sweden disagreed over who controlled the Aaland Islands.

Why was there a dispute between Sweden and Finland over the Aaland islands?

The peace settlement at the end of the war changed the geography of Europe and affected the borders of many countries. Both Sweden and Finland claimed the Aaland Islands. Historically, the islands were Finnish but the population wanted to be Swedish.

How did the League react to the dispute over the Aaland Islands?

The countries asked the League to investigate. It ruled that the islands should remain Finnish, but as a safeguard no military personnel or arms could be located there.

What was the result of the dispute over the Aaland Islands?

Both sides accepted the decision.

What was significant about the dispute between Sweden and Finland over the Aaland Islands?

The dispute over the Aaland Islands is a significant case study of success for the League of Nations. Both nations accepted the authority of the League and its decision.

THE DISPUTE OVER UPPER SILESIA, 1921

A plebiscite was supposed to decide whether a coal-mining region belonged to Germany or Poland...but did it?

What was the dispute in Upper Silesia?

The League became involved when there was a dispute between Germany and Poland in 1921 over Upper Silesia.

Where is Upper Silesia?

Upper Silesia was an industrial area on the border between Germany and Poland.

Who was involved in the dispute over Upper Silesia?

Poland and Germany disputed the territory in 1921. Upper Silesia was awarded to Poland in the Treaty of Versailles, but most of the region's population was German.

Why was there a dispute between Germany and Poland over Upper Silesia?

Upper Silesia was disputed by Poland and Germany for a number of reasons including:

- ☑ As a result of the Paris Peace Settlement, the boundaries of many countries were redrawn.
- ☑ Upper Silesia was on the border of Germany and Poland and both nationalities lived there, which caused conflict.
- ☑ It was also an important area for iron and steel production. Both countries wanted to make a claim on this.

What were the key events in the dispute between Germany and Poland over Upper Silesia?

There were a number of key events in the Upper Silesia crisis:

- ☑ In 1921 a plebiscite was organised by the League to decide whether Upper Silesia would become German or Polish territory. Britain and France sent troops to ensure the vote was democratic.
- ☑ Germany won 60% of the votes, but Poland argued that many of those that voted for Germany did not live in Upper Silesia.
- ☑ The League chose to split the area into regions based on the vote. Poland received many of the industrial areas, while Germany received the rural areas.
- ☑ At first this was accepted by both Poland and Germany.
- ☑ However, the final settlement was considered unfair by the Polish, who argued that Poland had half the population of Upper Silesia but only one third of the land.
- ☑ Germany claimed it had lost three quarters of the coal mines under the agreement.
- ☑ Germany complained to the League and was awarded the right to import coal at a discounted rate.

How did the League react to the dispute over Upper Silesia?

The League's actions included a plebiscite, investigations, consultation and measures to help improve the economic outlook of Poland and Germany.

What was the result of the dispute over Upper Silesia?

Both sides accepted the arrangements the League made regarding Upper Silesia, but they ended in 1925 and relations between Poland and Germany deteriorated.

What was significant about the dispute over Upper Silesia?

The dispute is a significant case study of success for the League. Both countries protested but were willing to accept the League's judgement, and therefore were able to find an acceptable compromise.

THE LEAGUE AND THE INVASION OF THE RUHR, 1923

The League didn't interfere when France invaded the German industrial region.

What was the dispute over the Ruhr?

In 1923, the League of Nations did not become involved in the dispute over the Ruhr.

Where is the Ruhr?

The Ruhr is an industrial region in north-west Germany.

Who was involved in the Ruhr dispute?

When Germany was unable to make its reparation payments in 1922, French and Belgian soldiers invaded the industrial Ruhr region in January 1923, and began to send goods to France as payment.

How did the League react to the Ruhr dispute?

Although this was an act of aggression by a stronger country against a weaker one, the League did nothing.

What was the result of the Ruhr dispute?

French troops did not leave the Ruhr until 1925. In the meantime, there was violence between them and German workers. The League of Nations appeared to only be interested in protecting the victors of the First World War.

THE CORFU INCIDENT, 1923

'The League is all very well when the sparrows shout, but no good at all when eagles fall out.'
Benito Mussolini

What was the Corfu dispute?

The dispute over the Greek island of Corfu in 1923, between Italy and Greece, was one of the most important disputes of the 1920s.

Where is Corfu?

Corfu is an island in the Mediterranean Sea and part of Greece.

Who was involved in the Corfu dispute?

The Corfu incident was part of a larger dispute between Italy and Greece.

Why did Italy and Greece argue over Corfu?

The invasion of Corfu was the result of an ongoing argument between Greece and Italy.

- Following the First World War, the border was redrawn between Greece and Albania. The Italian general, Tellini, had the job of patrolling it.
- In 1923, Tellini and some Italian soldiers were murdered on the border.
- In response the Italian fascist leader, Mussolini, demanded 50 million lira in compensation and the execution of those responsible. Greece refused.
- In retaliation, Italy invaded the Greek island of Corfu. Greece appealed to the League for help.

How did the League react to the Corfu dispute?

There were 4 important actions over Corfu:

- Italy did not accept action by the League in Corfu.
- The League responded quickly and ordered Italy to leave Corfu.
- Italy refused and demanded the question be passed to the Conference of Ambassadors, which was responsible for overseeing the peace settlement.
- The Conference of Ambassadors also ordered Italy to leave Corfu, but agreed that Greece should pay compensation.

What was the result of the Corfu dispute?

The Corfu dispute had a number of results.

- It revealed the League would give preferential treatment to powerful and aggressive members, like Italy.
- It led to the Geneva Protocol *(p.32)*, which was an attempt to make the League of Nations fairer.
- It also highlighted that when Britain and France did not stand united, they showed weakness.

What was significant about the dispute in Corfu between Italy and Greece?

The Corfu dispute was a significant case study of failure for the League for the following reasons:

- The incident showed the League was powerless against a bigger country which threatened a smaller country.
- It proved the League could be ignored and overruled by other international groups.

DID YOU KNOW?

Following the assassination of the Italian general by the Greeks, anti-Greek demonstrations broke out across Italy.

THE GENEVA PROTOCOL, 1924

Any country that refused to obey the League in a dispute would be recognised as an aggressor.

What was the Geneva Protocol?

The Geneva Protocol was a proposal drawn up in 1924 to strengthen collective security. It would make member states bring their disputes to the Permanent Court of International Justice for a ruling. They would have to accept it, or face economic or military sanctions. This would have made the League fairer and more united. However, it was never passed.

Who drew up the Geneva Protocol?

The proposal was drawn up by Britain and France.

What were the terms of the Geneva Protocol?

The Geneva Protocol had 4 important terms.

- ☑ The proposal contained suggestions to make the League of Nations fairer.
- ☑ The proposal outlined that if two members were to disagree, they would have to bring their dispute to the Permanent Court of International Justice for a hearing.
- ☑ They would then have to accept the ruling.
- ☑ If they didn't accept the ruling, they would face economic and military sanctions from the League of Nations.

Why wasn't the Geneva Protocol passed?

The Geneva Protocol failed for 3 important reasons:

- ☑ There was a change of government in Britain.
- ☑ The proposal was drawn up by the British Labour government, which was then voted out of power in the 1924 general election.
- ☑ The Labour Party was replaced by the British Conservative Party, which refused to sign it. The Conservatives were wary of Britain losing the ability to act in its own self-interest.

DID YOU KNOW?

The Labour government in Britain responsible for drafting the Geneva Protocol was only in power from January to November, 1924.

THE MOSUL DISPUTE, 1924

Turkey challenged Britain and Iraq for control of the city of Mosul.

What was the dispute over Mosul?

In 1924 the League of Nations became involved in a dispute over Mosul, in Iraq.

Where is Mosul?

The Mosul conflict was a dispute over the Kurdish region of Mosul, in Iraq.

Quizzes, amazing exam preparation tools and more at GCSEHistory.com

Who was involved in the Mosul dispute?

The Mosul dispute was between Iraq, alongside Britain which oversaw it as a mandate, and Turkey. In 1924, Turkey claimed the Kurdish-populated province of Mosul.

How did the League react to the Mosul dispute?

The League investigated and ruled Mosul should be returned to Iraq.

What was the result of the Mosul dispute?

Turkey accepted the judgement.

DID YOU KNOW?

Over 60% of the population in Mosul was Kurdish.
Turkey feared the rise of Kurdish nationalism in Iraq under British rule.

THE GREEK-BULGARIAN DISPUTE, 1925

Greek soldiers crossed the Bulgarian border.

What was the Greek-Bulgarian dispute?

The dispute between Greece and Bulgaria in 1925 was another test for the League.

Where did the Greek-Bulgarian dispute take place?

The dispute took place over the border between Greece and Bulgaria.

Who was involved in the Greek-Bulgarian dispute?

In October 1925 there was an incident on the Bulgarian border and, as a result, a Greek military officer was killed. Bulgaria appealed to the League for help when it was invaded by Greece.

Why was there a dispute between Greece and Bulgaria?

The dispute happened due to a shoot-out between Greek and Bulgarian soldiers on the Bulgarian border, resulting in the death of a Greek soldier. The Greeks invaded in retaliation.

How did the League react to the Greek-Bulgarian dispute?

There were 5 important ways the League reacted to the Greek invasion of Bulgaria.

- ☑ It reacted quickly to the invasion.
- ☑ It promptly called a meeting in Paris.
- ☑ It reached the decision that both sides should stand down, and Greek forces should leave Bulgaria immediately.
- ☑ After further investigation, the League decided it favoured Bulgaria's version of events.
- ☑ Greece was forced to pay £45,000 in compensation and threatened with sanctions.

What was the result of the Greek-Bulgarian dispute?

The Greeks complained the League had one rule for Italy, as during the Corfu *(p.30)* dispute, and another rule for them. They felt the League had been hypocritical but nevertheless agreed.

 What was significant about the dispute between Bulgaria and Greece?

The dispute between Greece and Bulgaria was significant as a case study of the failures of the League of Nations for the following reasons:

☑ It showed the League was inconsistent in its dealings with Greece, as Mussolini was allowed to take similar action during the incident in Corfu *(p.30)* in 1921.

☑ This suggested the League's reaction to disputes was dependent on the countries involved.

DID YOU KNOW?

The original incident that triggered the Greek invasion of Bulgaria was called 'the Petrich Incident', or 'the War of the Stray Dog'.

It apparently began in the border town of Petrich. A Greek soldier was shot dead as he ran towards Bulgarian lines, trying to stop and rescue his runaway dog.

INTERNATIONAL DIPLOMACY IN THE 1920S

'Nothing in the treaty impaired the covenant of the League of Nations...'
Henry Cabot Lodge

 What agreements were made between countries in the 1920s?

During the 1920s a number of agreements were made outside the League.

 What other agreements between countries were reached in the 1920s outside the League of Nations?

The most significant international agreements reached outside the League's influence were:

☑ The Washington Naval Agreement *(p.35)* of 1922.

☑ The Rapallo Treaty *(p.36)* of 1922.

☑ The Dawes Plan *(p.38)* of 1924.

☑ The Locarno Pact *(p.37)* of 1925.

☑ The Kellogg-Briand Pact of 1928.

☑ The Young Plan *(p.39)* of 1929.

 What was the significance of other agreements between countries in the 1920s on the League of Nations?

Diplomacy and agreements outside the League had a significant impact on it:

☑ They all involved nations which were not members of the League, and happened outside the League. This made the League look irrelevant.

☑ They showed that countries really trusted the League to keep the peace.

☑ They highlighted the problem that nations like the USA, Germany and the USSR were not members.

☑ They resulted in a growth of the League's reputation as a platform where grievances were aired and problems discussed, but no solutions were found.

DID YOU KNOW?

One of the most successful League commissions was the Health Organisation.

It is now known as the World Health Organisation, or WHO.

THE WASHINGTON NAVAL AGREEMENT, 1922

A first step towards disarmament?

What was the Washington Naval Agreement?

The Washington Naval Agreement was also known as the Five Power Naval Limitation Treaty. In it, the participants agreed limits on the size of their naval forces.

Why was the Washington Naval Agreement decided?

The Washington Naval Agreement was reached in order to reduce tension in the Asia-Pacific region.

When was the Washington Naval Agreement signed?

Negotiations for the Washington Naval Agreement began in 1921. It was finally signed on 6th February, 1922.

Where was the Washington Naval Agreement decided?

The Washington Naval Agreement was signed at the Washington Naval Conference. This is sometimes referred to as the International Conference of Naval Limitation.

Who was involved in the Washington Naval Agreement?

The conference where the agreement was decided upon was organised and hosted by the USA and attended by Britain, France, Italy and Japan. An additional agreement also involved Belgium, the Netherlands, Portugal, and China.

What were the terms agreed under the Washington Naval Agreement?

The agreement set out terms stating Britain and America could have equivalent navies. For every 5 tonnes their battleships weighed, Japan would be allowed 3 tonnes.

What was significant about the Washington Naval Agreement?

The agreement showed the League was not taken seriously for the following reasons:

☑ The League was committed to encouraging disarmament as one of its aims but was not involved in the first conference aimed at addressing this.

☑ Britain, France and Japan were 3 of the League's most powerful members, yet they attended the conference as individual countries rather than sending delegates through the League.

☑ The conference actually encouraged a new arms race in the building of lighter warships and submarines, and was the catalyst for a new naval building programme in the USA and Japan.

THE RAPALLO TREATY, 1922

It was between Germany and the USSR.

What was the Rapallo Treaty?

The Rapallo Treaty was an agreement between Germany and the USSR.

When was the Rapallo Treaty agreed between Germany and Russia?

The Rapallo Treaty was agreed in 1922.

Where was the Rapallo Treaty agreed between Germany and Russia?

The Rapallo Treaty was agreed at a meeting between representatives of Germany and the USSR in Rapallo, Italy.

Who was involved in the Rapallo Treaty?

The Rapallo Treaty was agreed between the USSR and Germany. At the time, neither were members of the League of Nations.

Why was the Rapallo Treaty agreed between Germany and the USSR?

There were 3 key reasons the treaty was agreed:

- ✅ Both countries wanted to rebuild their international presence.
- ✅ The USSR wanted to renegotiate the 1918 Treaty of Brest-Litovsk, which had seen the vast annexation of Soviet land by Germany.
- ✅ The USSR was also forced to make huge reparation payments to Germany under the Treaty of Brest-Litovsk.

What were the results of the Rapallo Treaty?

Germany agreed to return the reparations and land taken under the Treaty of Brest-Litovsk to the USSR. Both countries also agreed to cooperate in the future.

What was significant about the Rapallo Treaty agreed between Germany and Russia?

The Rapallo Treaty was significant because it undermined the work of the League. It was supposed to lead the way in encouraging cooperation between countries, yet the League was not involved at all.

THE LOCARNO PACT, 1925

France and Germany settled their differences, along with Britain, Belgium and Italy.

What was the Locarno Pact?

The Locarno Pact was a treaty intended to improve the relationship between Germany, Belgium and France by protecting their borders.

When was the Locarno Pact signed?

The Locarno Pact was signed in December 1925.

Who signed the Locarno Pact?

The pact was signed by Germany, Belgium, France, Britain and Italy.

Why was the Locarno Pact signed?

It was intended to improve the relationship between Germany and her neighbours. German leader, Gustav Stresemann, also wanted to prevent them from being invaded again after the French and Belgian occupation of the Ruhr in 1923.

What were the terms of the Locarno Pact?

There were 5 key terms of the Locarno Pact:

- ✅ Germany accepted its new borders with France, drawn up under the Treaty of Versailles. France pledged peace with Germany; it would not occupy Germany again.
- ✅ Germany accepted its new borders with Belgium, drawn up under the Treaty of Versailles, and Belgium pledged peace with Germany.
- ✅ If there was a border dispute between Germany and France or Germany and Belgium, Britain and Italy would step in as guarantors to solve the problems.
- ✅ The five countries agreed to discuss Germany's membership of the League of Nations.
- ✅ It was agreed the Rhineland would be permanently demilitarised.

What were the benefits of the Locarno Pact?

There were 4 key benefits of the Locarno Pact:

- ✅ War was less likely because the relationships between Germany, France, Britain, Belgium and Italy improved.
- ✅ Germany was treated like an equal, rather than the loser of the First World War.
- ✅ As the Locarno Pact had been negotiated between Germany and the other countries, unlike the Treaty of Versailles, it was more acceptable to the public. It improved the reputation of the government and increased support for the moderate political parties.
- ✅ It paved the way for Germany to join the League of Nations.

What were the criticisms of the Locarno Pact?

The drawback of the Locarno Pact was that extremist political parties hated it, primarily because it confirmed the borders laid out in the detested Treaty of Versailles.

What was significant about the Locarno Pact to the League of Nations?

The Locarno pact was significant to the League of Nations for both positive and negative reasons:

- ✅ Positively, the pact paved the way for Germany to join the League - in order for the organisation to be effective, it was important as many countries as possible supported its work.

☑ On the negative side, it can be considered a failure of the League. The organisation should have led international agreements regarding peace, but was not involved in this pact.

THE DAWES PLAN, 1924

A system of loans between America and Germany.

What was the Dawes Plan?

The Dawes Plan was an agreement between the USA and Weimar Germany which helped to solve Germany's problems in paying reparations.

When was the Dawes Plan signed?

The Dawes Plan was negotiated in April 1924 and signed in October 1924.

Who created the Dawes Plan?

The Dawes Plan was created by American banker, Charles G Dawes, along with Gustav Stresemann.

Why was the Dawes Plan created?

The Dawes Plan was created to solve Germany's problems in paying reparations following the 1923 hyperinflation crisis.

What was agreed in the Dawes Plan?

The Dawes Plan included 3 key terms:

☑ A temporary reduction in the annual reparations repayments to £50 million.

☑ US banks and businesses offered loans worth 800 million marks to German industries and businesses.

☑ The German State Bank, the Reichsbank, should be reorganised and supervised by the Allies.

What were the benefits of the Dawes Plan?

There were 3 main benefits of the Dawes Plan:

☑ American loans helped industrial output to double between 1923 and 1928. Employment, income tax and trade all increased as a result.

☑ The French and Belgians left the Ruhr as they were promised that they would receive reparations as result of the Dawes Plan.

☑ The Weimar Republic became politically stronger as the economy improved.

What were the criticisms of the Dawes Plan?

There were 2 key criticisms of the Dawes Plan:

☑ In the short-term, both the extreme left-wing and extreme right-wing political parties were angry Germany was still paying reparations imposed by the Treaty of Versailles.

✅ In the long term, because the Weimar economy was dependent on US loans, Germany could be economically damaged if these were suddenly recalled.

DID YOU KNOW?

Adolf Hitler attacked the Dawes Plan on the grounds it didn't actually reduce the amount of reparations.

THE YOUNG PLAN, 1929

It extended the principles of the Dawes Plan.

What was the Young Plan?

The Young Plan was another deal that aimed to help Germany pay the reparations bill.

When was the Young Plan created?

The Young Plan was signed in August 1929.

Who created the Young Plan?

Owen Young, an American banker, helped negotiate the Young Plan with Stresemann and Germany.

Why was the Young Plan needed?

The Young Plan was created to help Weimar Germany pay its reparations bill.

What was agreed in the Young Plan?

The Young Plan stated Germany would have 59 years to pay the reparations bill, which was reduced from £6.6 billion to £2 billion.

What were the benefits of the Young Plan?

There were 3 key benefits of the Young Plan:

✅ The lower reparations payments meant the Weimar government could in turn reduce taxes, giving people more money to spend or save.

✅ It helped them recover economically.

✅ It increased confidence politically.

How did the Young Plan not help Weimar Germany?

There were 2 key criticisms of the Young Plan:

✅ The reparations payment was still high at £50 million per year.

✅ The extreme political parties were furious that reparations had not been cancelled. Hitler commented that extending payments over 59 years was "passing the penalty onto the unborn.".

THE LEAGUE OF NATIONS AND THE GREAT DEPRESSION

Economic hardship made peace more difficult.

What was the effect of the Great Depression on the League of Nations?

The Great Depression affected attitudes towards international relations, peace, aggression, and the League of Nations.

How did the Great Depression affect attitudes towards sanctions by the League of Nations?

Members of the League were not keen to impose economic sanctions because they were worried about losing trade.

How did the Great Depression lead to the rise of extremism?

The poverty and unemployment in nations created by the Great Depression led to support for political parties that promised extreme solutions. A key example is the Nazi party in Germany.

How did the Great Depression lead to the rise of militarism?

Nations became more likely to use military force to protect their economies and trade. For example, the Japanese army began to behave more aggressively in 1931.

How did the Great Depression lead attitudes towards territory?

Nations wanted to find new resources and markets to boost their economies. This meant they were more likely to try and take land belonging to other countries.

How did the Great Depression affect attitudes towards armament?

The League was committed to disarmament, but also relied on member armies to help carry out its work. The Great Depression affected armament in 2 ways:

- ☑ Governments were under pressure to cut spending on armies and weapons. The League's members didn't have the military power to deal with aggressors.
- ☑ As a result of the Great Depression, many governments, such as Germany's, turned to rearmament as a way of offering more stability and jobs in a time of crisis.

THE LEAGUE OF NATIONS IN THE 1930S

A turn for the worse.

 ### What were the 1930s like for the League of Nations?

The 1930s were disastrous for the League, and it was ultimately shown to be a failure with the outbreak of the Second World War in 1939.

 ### What did the League of Nations achieve in the 1930s?

The League did achieve a few positive changes in the 1930s.

- ☑ The commissions continued to solve problems and do good work.
- ☑ The Saar Commission successfully held the Saar plebiscite in 1935.
- ☑ The League helped solve some border disputes in South America.

What were the League of Nation's failures in the 1930s?

The League suffered some disastrous failures in the 1930s.

- ☑ The Japanese invasion of Manchuria.
- ☑ The World Disarmament Conference.
- ☑ The Italian invasion of Abyssinia *(p.44)* by Mussolini.
- ☑ The secret Hoare-Laval agreement over Abyssinia *(p.44)*.

DID YOU KNOW?

In 1936, the League was successful in getting 26 countries to sign an agreement to stop the international drugs trade.

THE MANCHURIAN CRISIS, 1931

'Let the League of Nations say whatever it pleases... Japan must adhere to its course unswervingly.'
Sadao Araki

 ### What was the Manchurian Crisis?

In 1931 the League faced its most serious challenge yet, when Japan invaded the Chinese province of Manchuria.

 ### Where is Manchuria?

Manchuria is a province of north-east China. It had a sparse population but was rich in minerals, agricultural land and forestry. It bordered Korea, which was controlled by Japan.

 ### Why did Japan invade Manchuria in 1931?

In 1931 Japanese troops invaded Manchuria. There were a number of reasons for this, both economic and political:

- ☑ Japan had suffered badly in the Depression, as it had few natural resources and its main export was silk.
- ☑ Japan exported much of its silk to rich countries, like America, but the impact of the Depression meant people were not buying luxury goods. By 1932 silk was worth one fifth of its value in 1920. Production and employment had fallen by 30% by 1930.

- Japan started to look for land and resources elsewhere to minimise the impact of the depression.
- Japan already had large industries and a railway line through Manchuria, and guards to protect it. Japan was worried China might expel Japanese industry.
- The Japanese government wanted to take the land to upset its old enemy, Russia, and use that as a way to distract people from its domestic problems.
- Japan wanted to seize the opportunity while the Japanese army was growing stronger and Chinese power was weakening.
- In September 1931 there was an explosion on the Manchurian railway in Mukden. This is believed to have been set up by the Japanese army, but the Japanese blamed Chinese bandits. This became known as the Mukden Incident.
- The Japanese army was stronger than its civilian government and took control, marching into Manchuria and taking over.

What happened when Japan invaded Manchuria?

By March 1932 the Japanese army had invaded the whole province of Manchuria and renamed it Manchukuo. The Chinese emperor, Pu Yi, was installed as a puppet leader controlled by the Japanese.

Why was the League of Nations reluctant to act over the Manchurian crisis at first?

This incident looked like a clear case of aggression as Japan had invaded Manchuria and was in the wrong. However, the League was reluctant to act for a number of reasons:

- Many argued that Japan owned Manchuria and was entitled to take control. China had previously agreed economic rights in the area.
- China and Japan were seen as a long way away from the League's headquarters in Geneva. Britain and France felt it was too far away to be a concern to them.
- Japan was a powerful member of the League, there was a lot of confusion surrounding the Mukden Incident and there was a convincing argument that China had attacked Japan first.
- China was very disorganised and some people thought it was a good thing Japan had invaded the region. It was seen by some as protection against communism.

How did the League respond to the invasion of Manchuria?

China appealed to the League and called upon it to act.

- At first, the League issued a moral condemnation and told Japan to remove its troops. The Japanese refused and there was not much the League could do.
- The next tool at their disposal was to issue economic sanctions. However, Japan's biggest trading relationship was with the USA, who was not a member of the League. This would therefore be pointless.
- Geographically, Manchuria was far away from the League's more powerful members. The nearest powerful country was the Soviet Union, but it was not a member of the League and could not be called upon for help.
- The League could use military action but members would not send their armies as they could not afford to fight someone else's battle so far away in the midst of a depression.
- The League didn't want to do nothing, so it appointed Lord Lytton to lead a commission of inquiry into Manchuria.

What did the Lytton Commission do in Manchuria?

The Lytton Commission spent six weeks investigating in the province and concluded the invasion was not justified. It presented its findings in the Lytton report.

What decisions did the League of Nations reach about Manchuria?

The League considered the findings in February 1933 and accepted them by 42 to 1, but failed to impose economic or military sanctions. By this point the crisis had lasted for 18 months and many people criticised the League for being too slow to act.

What were the results of the Manchurian Crisis?

There were a number of results to the League's actions in Manchuria:

- ☑ In response to the League's judgement, Japan left the organisation and continued to occupy Manchuria.
- ☑ The League looked ineffective and slow.
- ☑ In 1933 Japan invaded the Chinese province of Jehol, and launched a full-scale invasion of China in 1937.

What was the significance of the Manchurian crisis for the League of Nations?

The Manchurian crisis was significant because the League had failed. One of its members had broken the rules, but the League was slow to react and did little. The crisis demonstrated the League was weak and indecisive, and that powerful countries could get away with aggression.

DID YOU KNOW?

The Lytton Commission had four other members apart from Lord Lytton.

They were representatives of the USA, Germany, France and Italy.

THE WORLD DISARMAMENT CONFERENCE, 1932

'The world wants disarmament. The world needs disarmament.'
Arthur Henderson

What was the World Disarmament Conference?

Between 1932 and 1934, a World Disarmament Conference was run by the Disarmament Commission in Geneva.

Why was the World Disarmament Conference held?

One of the main aims of the League was to encourage disarmament. However, it had failed at this in the 1920s. There was growing pressure for disarmament in the 1930s for 2 key reasons:

- ☑ The Japanese invasion of Manchuria had shown the League was weak against powerful countries with a large military force. Japanese military strength was also increasing.
- ☑ Hitler had recently been elected to power on a pledge of work and bread by rebuilding Germany's army. The League was afraid of the increasing military strength of countries like Germany and Italy.

What were the key events of the World Disarmament Conference?

The first meeting for disarmament took place in July 1932, even though some countries were still unwilling to disarm. There were 5 key events:

- ☑ Germany began by putting forward the idea that all countries should disarm to the same level as Germany. However, this upset the French.
- ☑ By December 1932 all attendees had agreed to treat Germany as an equal. The League was optimistic about reaching an agreement.
- ☑ However, this changed in 1933 when Hitler was elected as chancellor of Germany and began to secretly rearm the nation.
- ☑ At the conference in May 1933, Hitler promised not to rearm Germany if all other countries destroyed their arms within 5 years. In October 1933, France refused.
- ☑ Following this, Germany left the League of Nations in November 1933.

Why did countries disagree at the World Disarmament Conference?

The World Disarmament Conference failed to reach any decisions, as many individual states were anxious about their own internal troubles.

- France was mostly unwilling to disarm, but might have been prepared to do so had it received guarantees from the US and Britain. However, neither country would do this.
- Hitler came to power in Germany in 1933, and accused France of failing to take disarmament seriously. He used it as an excuse to leave the conference altogether.
- Japan left the League during the conference as a result of the Manchurian Crisis *(p.41)*, and it became apparent disarmament was unlikely.
- The German delegates walked out early in the talks because their country wasn't treated equally by the other members. They returned, but Germany began to rearm secretly.
- France, Poland and Czechoslovakia were already worried about the German threat and the League's protection looked increasingly insecure.

 What was the impact of the World Disarmament Conference on the League of Nations?

The failure of the conference led people to question the League's efficacy. It was supposedly committed to reducing arms, but it took more than ten years to bring leaders together to discuss the issue, and members then left the League when talks broke down.

DID YOU KNOW?

Public opinion for disarmament was strong.
The British Women's Society received 8 million signatures in favour of disarmament.

THE ABYSSINIAN CRISIS, 1935

'God and history will remember your judgement.'
Haile Selassie

 What was the Abyssinian Crisis?

The Abyssinian Crisis occurred from 1935 to 1936, when Italy invaded the independent country of Abyssinia in East Africa.

 Where is Abyssinia?

Abyssinia is now called Ethiopia and is located on the north-east coast of Africa. In 1935 it was surrounded by British, French and Italian colonies, but remained independent.

 Why did Italy invade Abyssinia?

Italy, led by the fascist government of Mussolini since 1922, had several reasons for wanting to control Abyssinia:

- Italy owned Italian Somaliland and Eritrea, territories on either side of Abyssinia.
- In 1896, the Abyssinians defeated the Italians at Adowa. The Italians were humiliated and wanted revenge.
- Abyssinia was rich in natural resources and had fertile land for livestock which would help the Italian economy.
- Mussolini was seeking glory and conquest, attempting to bring the Roman Empire back to Italy. He didn't think Britain and France could argue when they had such vast empires themselves.

- Italy felt sure of victory. It had a modern army while Abyssinian soldiers were armed with spears and arrows.
- Mussolini was confident he could invade Abyssinia without the League taking action, based on his previous actions in Corfu *(p.30)* in 1923 and the League's failure in Manchuria.
- Mussolini was confident Britain and France wouldn't stop him establishing an empire in Africa. He felt Britain and France would do anything to keep Italy as an ally against Germany, especially after the Stresa Front of 1935.

What happened at the invasion in the Abyssinian Crisis?

Mussolini's chance for invasion came in 1934:

- In December 1934 there was a border incident at Wal Wal in Abyssinia. Italian soldiers clashed with Abyssinians on Mussolini's commands; two Italians and 150 Abyssinians were killed.
- The League wanted to get involved but found it hard to stop Mussolini. Both nations were members of the League, but Mussolini was set on war.
- In January 1935 the French foreign minister, Pierre Laval, met with Mussolini and made a top secret deal - the Hoare-Laval Pact.
- Italy began to build up forces in Eritrea and Somaliland. In October 1935 an attack was launched involving 250,000 men.
- The League next issued Italy with a moral condemnation, which Mussolini ignored.

What were Italy's international relations like before the Abyssinian Crisis?

Before the crisis of 1935, Italy had worked with Britain and France in the war, the peace conference, and the League. In April 1935 the countries formed the Stresa Pact against German aggression.

How did the League respond to the invasion of Abyssinia?

The invasion of Abyssinia was clearly an aggressive act by a strong country against a weaker one. On 30th June 1935, Abyssinian emperor Haile Selassie addressed the League, warning it of the effects of its failures.

- The League placed economic sanctions on Italy.
- However, it didn't sanction oil, coal, iron or steel; essential resources for war.
- The Suez Canal, which was owned by Britain and France, provided a short-cut from the Mediterranean to East Africa but wasn't closed. Britain and France didn't want to risk conflict with Italy, but this allowed it to build up men and supplies near Abyssinia more quickly.

How did Britain and France respond to the Italian invasion of Abyssinia?

Britain and France responded in the following ways:

- Britain and France wanted to avoid embarrassment over Abyssinia, so they began to secretly negotiate with Italy without consulting Haile Selassie, the Abyssinian emperor.
- The British public wanted to protect Abyssinia, and British politicians made strong speeches about standing up to aggression.
- However, in secret, the British and French foreign ministers negotiated the Hoare-Laval Pact with Mussolini. This would give two thirds of Abyssinia to Italy, leaving the Abyssinians with only the mountainous regions.
- The details of the Hoare-Laval Pact were leaked and the public was horrified. The plan was dropped, but Italy continued to invade Abyssinia.

What were the results of the Abyssinian Crisis?

The League's reputation was already badly damaged after the Manchurian Crisis *(p.41)*, but the Abyssinian Crisis of 1935-36 offered final proof of the failure of collective security.

- Italy completed the invasion of Abyssinia with the capture of Addis Ababa in May 1936.
- Sanctions on Italy were lifted in July 1936.
- The Abyssinian Crisis proved that Britain and France prioritised other concerns above the principles of the League.

- ☑ Adolf Hitler observed the lack of decisive action in response to aggression. This may have informed his future decisions.
- ☑ Italy was offended by the imposition of sanctions, and left the League in 1937.
- ☑ The League of Nations never recovered its reputation or influence.

Why did the League fail in Abyssinia?

The League failed to deal with the crisis in Abyssinia for several reasons:

- ☑ Britain and France were too concerned about upsetting Mussolini and losing a potential ally against Germany. They didn't close down the Suez Canal, even though this could have stopped Mussolini.
- ☑ The economic trade sanctions against Italy were too slow and were limited by the non-membership of wealthy trading states, such as the USA. Self-interest from the League's members also prevented a ban on some goods.
- ☑ The Hoare-Laval Pact again demonstrated that Britain and France were looking after their own interests.
- ☑ The League also banned members from selling arms to Abyssinia, so the country could not even defend itself against Italy.

Why did the League's economic sanctions fail in the Abyssinian Crisis?

The League's economic sanctions against Italy were ineffective because the trade of some key goods could not be prevented.

- ☑ Britain didn't want to sanction its coal exports to Italy as this might cause unemployment for British miners.
- ☑ Even if oil sales to Italy had been stopped by the League, the USA would have continued to sell to it as a non-member.
- ☑ Mussolini stated afterwards that a ban on coal and oil sales to Italy would have stopped his invasion.

What was the significance of the Abyssinian Crisis to the League of Nations?

The Abyssinian Crisis was significant as it could be considered the main reason for the final downfall of the League.

- ☑ Britain and France had proved they were more interested in their own national concerns than protecting the aims of the League.
- ☑ Small countries knew the League could provide them with no real protection from aggressive countries.
- ☑ The League lost all respect and its reputation was damaged beyond repair. Although it continued to run, it was no longer considered a serious force in international relations.

DID YOU KNOW?

The last emperor of Abyssinia, Haile Selassie, is seen as a god by Rastafarians.

THE LEAGUE OF NATIONS AFTER 1936

'We went to the League building, which is a vast affair, a huge modern, white, dignified, lavish, empty palace...'
Chips Channon, 1938

What did the League of Nations do after 1936?

After 1936 the League really existed in name only. Its reputation was destroyed and it played no part in international relations.

What did the League of Nations do about Hitler after 1936?

The causes of the Second World War were a complex combination of multiple factors. The League, however, had shown Hitler that aggressive nations could go unchecked.

 ### What did the League of Nations do after 1936?

There were no council or assembly *(p.19)* meetings of the League during the Second World War. It met for the final time in April 1946.

 ### What were the contributions of the League of Nations' commissions after 1936?

The commissions and other elements of the League of Nations were successful and influential after 1936, despite the failure of the League itself.

- ☑ Ideas such as the Permanent Court of Justice *(p.20)* and International Labour Organisation *(p.21)* were built into the United Nations.
- ☑ The Health Organisation became the World Health Organisation and continues to this day.

DID YOU KNOW?

The League of Nations was officially closed down in 1946.

A

Abolish, Abolished - to stop something, or get rid of it.

Abolition - the act of abolishing something, i.e. to stop or get rid of it.

Aggression - angry, hostile or violent behaviour displayed without provocation.

Agricultural - relating to agriculture.

Allies - parties working together for a common objective, such as countries involved in a war. In both world wars, 'Allies' refers to those countries on the side of Great Britain.

Annex, Annexation, Annexed - to forcibly acquire territory and add it to a larger country.

Assembly - a meeting of a group of people, often as part of a country's government, to make decisions.

B

Bankrupt - to be insolvent; to have run out of resources with which to pay existing debts.

Blacklist - the blocking of trade as a means to punish.

C

Campaign - a political movement to get something changed; in military terms, it refers to a series of operations to achieve a goal.

Casualties - people who have been injured or killed, such as during a war, accident or catastrophe.

Chancellor - a senior state official who, in some countries, is the head of the government and responsible for the day-to-day running of the nation.

Civil servant - a person who works for the government, either at national or local level.

Civilian - a non-military person.

Claim - someone's assertion of their right to something - for example, a claim to the throne.

Collective security - a policy adopted by the League of Nations, with the idea members should feel safe from attack as all nations agreed to defend each other.

Colonies, Colony - a country or area controlled by another country and occupied by settlers.

Commissions - the collective term for several organisations set up by the League of Nations to solve global issues.

Communism - the belief, based on the ideas of Karl Marx, that all people should be equal in society without government, money or private property. Everything is owned by by the people, and each person receives according to need.

Communist - a believer in communism.

Conference - a formal meeting to discuss common issues of interest or concern.

Constitution - rules, laws or principles that set out how a country is governed.

Constitutional - relating to the constitution.

Cooperate, Cooperation - to work together to achieve a common aim. Frequently used in relation to politics, economics or law.

Council - an advisory or administrative body set up to manage the affairs of a place or organisation. The Council of the League of Nations contained the organisation's most powerful members.

Credit - the ability to borrow money, or use goods or services, on the understanding that it will be paid for later.

Currency - an umbrella term for any form of legal tender, but most commonly referring to money.

D

Demilitarised - to remove all military forces from an area and forbid them to be stationed there.

Democratic - relating to or supporting the principles of democracy.

Disarm - to remove any land, sea and air weaponry.

Disarmament - the reduction or removal of weaponry.

Dispute - a disagreement or argument; often used to describe conflict between different countries.

Dissolution, Dissolve - the formal ending of a partnership, organisation or official body.

Dysentery - an intestinal infection that causes diarrhoea containing blood or mucus. Other symptoms can include stomach cramps, nausea and vomiting. In some cases it can lead to death due to severe dehydration.

E

Economic - relating to the economy; also used when justifying something in terms of profitability.

Economy - a country, state or region's position in terms of production and consumption of goods and services, and the supply of money.

Electorate - a group of people who are eligible to vote.

Empire - a group of states or countries ruled over and controlled by a single monarch.

Epidemic - an outbreak of disease that spreads quickly and affects many individuals at the same time.

Eradicate, Eradication - to destroy something and completely wipe it out.

Export - to transport goods for sale to another country.

Extreme - furthest from the centre or any given point. If someone holds extreme views, they are not moderate and are considered radical.

F

Fascist - one who believes in fascism.

H

Hygiene, Hygienic - a term for conditions or practices with the aim of maintaining good health and preventing disease, especially in regard to cleanliness.

Hyperinflation - rapid acceleration of inflation which typically sees a currency lose its value and become worthless. As a result, the price of goods skyrockets for a short period of time.

I

Import - to bring goods or services into a different country to sell.

Independence, Independent - to be free of control, often meaning by another country, allowing the people of a nation the ability to govern themselves.

Industrial - related to industry, manufacturing and/or production.

Industry - the part of the economy concerned with turning raw materials into into manufactured goods, for example making furniture from wood.

International relations - the relationships between different countries.

Isolationism - a policy adopted by the USA after the First World War which saw them withdraw from international disputes and European politics.

L

Left wing - used to describe political groups or individuals with beliefs that are usually centered around socialism and the idea of reform.

Leprosy - a contagious and painful disease affecting the skin, mucous membranes and nerves; it can lead to permanent damage and even death.

M

Mandate - authority to carry out a policy.

Military force - the use of armed forces.

Mine - an explosive device usually hidden underground or underwater.

Minister - a senior member of government, usually responsible for a particular area such as education or finance.

Moderate - someone who is not extreme.

Morals - a person's set of rules about what they consider right and wrong, used to guide their actions and behaviour.

O

Occupation - the action, state or period when somewhere is taken over and occupied by a military force.

P

POW, Prisoner of war, Prisoners of war - somebody who has been captured and taken prisoner by enemy forces.

Parliament - a group of politicians who make the laws of their country, usually elected by the population.

Plebiscite - a vote or referendum on an important matter in an area or country.

Population - the number of people who live in a specified place.

Poverty - the state of being extremely poor.

President - the elected head of state of a republic.

Prevent, Preventative, Preventive - steps taken to stop something from happening.

Production - a term used to describe how much of something is made, for example saying a factory has a high production rate.

Province, Provinces - part of an empire or a country denoting areas that have been divided for administrative purposes.

R

Raid - a quick surprise attack on the enemy.

Refugee, Refugees - a person who has been forced to leave where they live due to war, disaster or persecution.

Reparations - payments made by the defeated countries in a war to the victors to help pay for the cost of and damage from the fighting.

Right wing - a political view with beliefs centred around nationalism and a desire for an authoritarian government opposed to communism.

S

Sanctions - actions taken against states who break international laws, such as a refusal to trade with them or supply necessary commodities.

Smallpox - a contagious and potentially fatal disease that causes a high fever, rashes and blisters.

Socialist - one who believes in the principles of socialism.

Soviet - an elected workers' council at local, regional or national level in the former Soviet Union. It can also be a reference to the Soviet Union or the USSR.

State, States - an area of land or a territory ruled by one government.

T

Territories, Territory - an area of land under the control of a ruler/ country.

Treaty - a formal agreement, signed and ratified by two or more parties.

U

Unanimity, Unanimous - when everyone involved is fully in agreement with each other.

V

Veto - the right to reject a decision or proposal.

Quizzes, amazing exam preparation tools and more at GCSEHistory.com